a b c d e f g h i j k l m n o p q r s t u v w x y z

What comes between?

m ___ o

r ___ t

n ___ p

c ___ e

s ___ u

p ___ r

w ___ y

b ___ d

e ___ g

l ___ n

T0204751

a b c d e f g h i j k l m n o p q r s t u v w x y z

What's missing?

p ___ ___ s

j ___ l ___

___ h ___ j

d ___ ___ ___ g

m ___ ___ ___ p

___ e f ___

g ___ i ___

r ___ ___ ___ u

a b ___ ___ ___

l ___ n ___

v ___ ___ ___ y

4

BEGINNING DICTIONARY

Written and Illustrated by
Eleanor Villalpando

ISBN# 1-56175-086-7

REMEDIA PUBLICATIONS   **10135 E. VIA LINDA, #D124**   **SCOTTSDALE, AZ 85258**
Toll Free 1-800-826-4740   **FAX 602-661-9901**

Beginning Dictionary Skills
Introduction

This book is intended to provide practice in alphabetizing and using the dictionary after each concept has been taught by the teacher and reinforced with some group activity. The activities have been developed around the contents of beginning dictionaries available from several different publishers.

It is suggested that children work as a group with teacher supervision as each new step is introduced. Once they understand the concept, these activities will offer independent practice and further reinforcement of the skill.

Activities progress in level of difficulty from putting single letters in alphabetical order to ordering words by the second letter. Once children grasp this idea, the progression to third and fourth letters is almost automatic.

Dictionary activities are designed to build comfort and familiarity with the use of this book. The practice begins with sectioning the dictionary into thirds using the alphabet.

Students then begin practice in finding specific words and noting only page numbers. Once they have developed some facility in locating words, they are ready to use what they find. Activities follow on parts of speech and the use of word meanings.

The final exercises touch on multiple meanings when the same word appears as two entry words, each having a specific definition.

Upon completion of teacher instruction, group reinforcement, and independent practice, students should be comfortable with using a dictionary and be ready to use it as a reference tool in their daily work.

ε 1990 REMEDIA PUBLICATIONS

a b c d e f g h i j k l m n o p q r s t u v w x y z

What comes next?

d _____
r _____
f _____

v _____
i _____
a _____

m _____
b _____
y _____

l _____
t _____
c _____

g _____
p _____
w _____

o _____
j _____
q _____

e _____
h _____
u _____

a b c d e f g h i j k l m n o p q r s t u v w x y z

What comes before?

Name _____

Alphabetizing

What am I?

Use the ABC's to follow the dots. Color the picture.

© 1990 REMEDIA PUBLICATIONS

5

What am I?

Use the ABC's to follow the dots. Color the picture.

© 1990 REMEDIA PUBLICATIONS

Put the letters in ABC order.

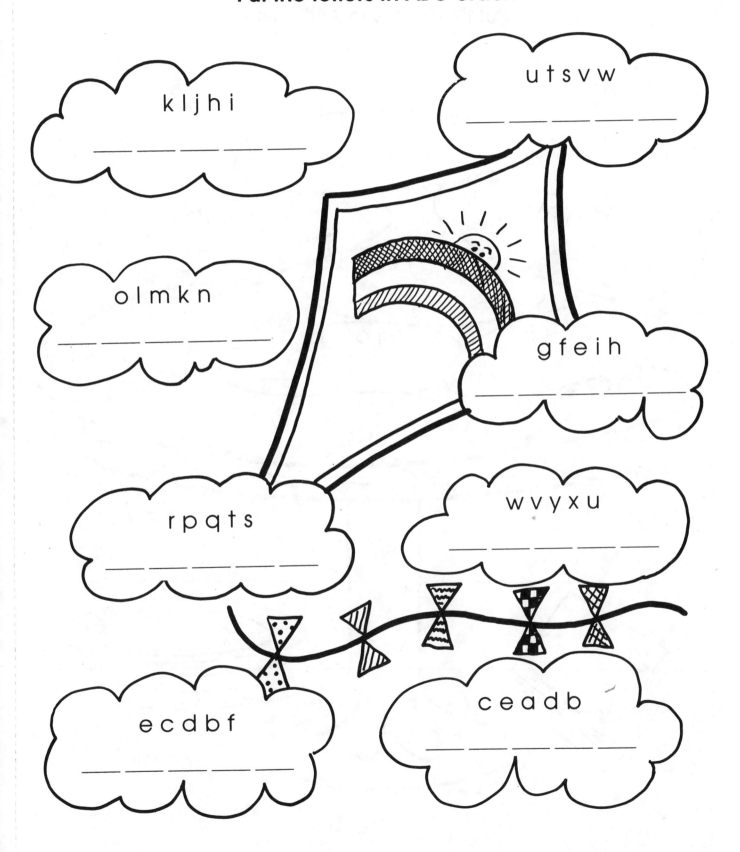

k l j h i
_____

u t s v w
_____

o l m k n
_____

g f e i h
_____

r p q t s
_____

w v y x u
_____

e c d b f
_____

c e a d b
_____

Put the letters in ABC order.

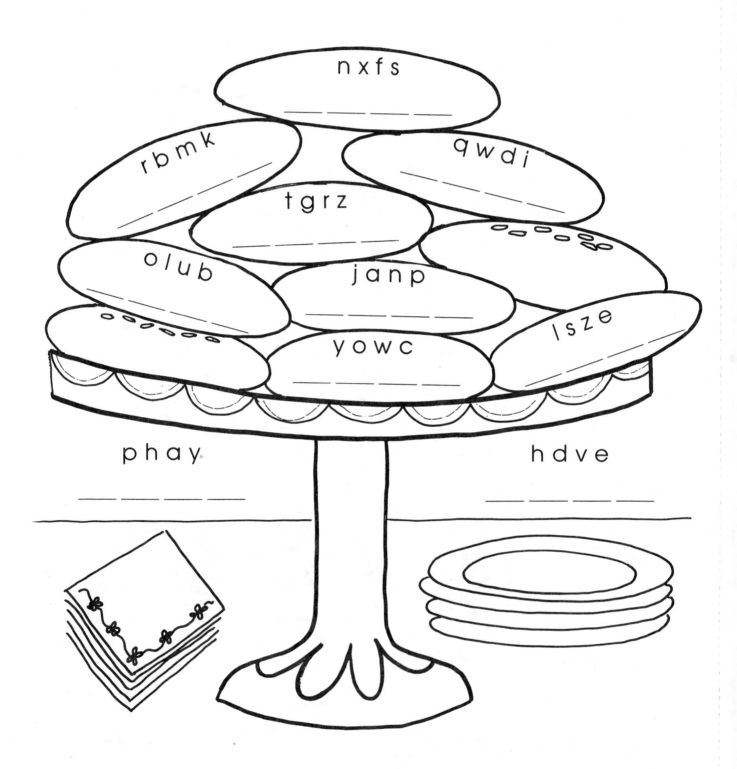

Name _____   **Alphabetizing**

Which would come first?

Write it on the line.

up down	in out	black white
_____	_____	_____
day night	sad happy	cute ugly
_____	_____	_____
go come	bring take	new old
_____	_____	_____
tall short	cold hot	thin fat
_____	_____	_____
boy girl	hard soft	high low
_____	_____	_____

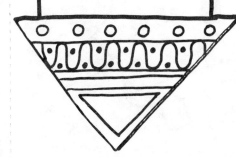

Put the letters in ABC order.

Name _____

Write the words in ABC order.

bed
did
cat

_____
_____
_____

into
just
hop

_____
_____
_____

man
let
nice

_____
_____
_____

not
pin
off

_____
_____
_____

hat
fly
give

_____
_____
_____

11

Name _____

Number the words in ABC order.

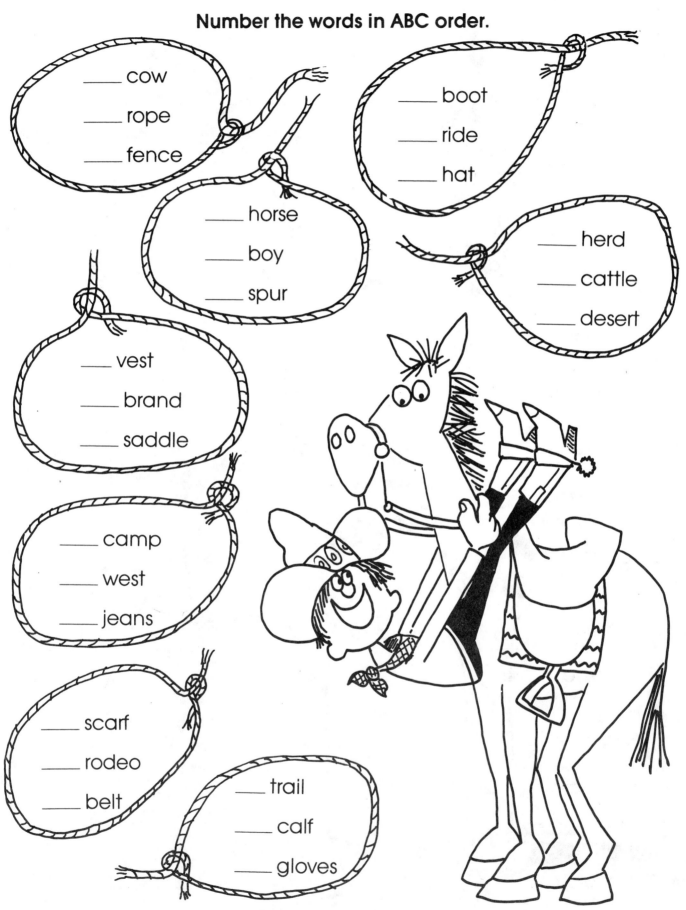

____ cow
____ rope
____ fence

____ boot
____ ride
____ hat

____ horse
____ boy
____ spur

____ herd
____ cattle
____ desert

____ vest
____ brand
____ saddle

____ camp
____ west
____ jeans

____ scarf
____ rodeo
____ belt

____ trail
____ calf
____ gloves

12

© 1990 REMEDIA PUBLICATIONS

Number the words in ABC order.

___ soap	___ candy	___ carrots
___ cereal	___ juice	___ salt
___ lettuce	___ apples	___ butter
___ milk	___ ice	___ ketchup
___ rice	___ soup	___ tissues
___ cheese	___ crackers	___ cookies
___ bleach	___ bread	___ bananas
___ oranges	___ pepper	___ nuts
___ tea	___ oil	___ sugar
___ hot dogs	___ yogurt	___ tomatoes
___ celery	___ coffee	___ donuts
___ buns	___ flour	___ chips
___ potatoes	___ beans	___ ham
___ noodles	___ meat	___ peas
___ tuna	___ peaches	___ onions

Name _____   **Alphabetizing**

Number the words in ABC order.

___ town
___ state
___ map
___ east
___ west

___ day
___ night
___ time
___ week
___ month

___ one
___ four
___ ten
___ seven
___ eight

___ glad
___ sad
___ happy
___ upset
___ angry

___ run
___ jump
___ hop
___ skip
___ walk

___ yell
___ talk
___ shout
___ cry
___ laugh

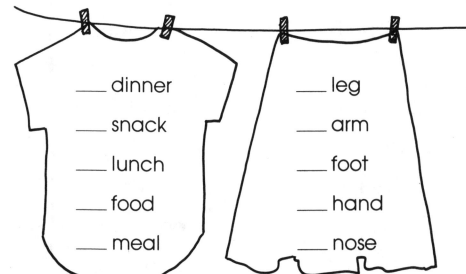

___ dinner
___ snack
___ lunch
___ food
___ meal

___ leg
___ arm
___ foot
___ hand
___ nose

14

Write the words in ABC order. They will make a sentence.

1. soccer Boys play can.

    _____

    _____

2. likes A worms skinny fish.

    _____

    _____

3. long giraffes necks All have.

    _____

    _____

4. the Fred pulling weeds is.

    _____

    _____

5. saw How people you many?

    _____

    _____

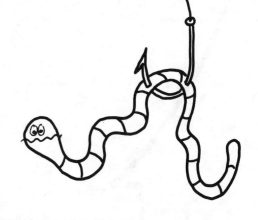

Write the words in ABC order. They will make a sentence.

1. sick Don today feels.

    _____

    _____

2. elephant peanuts likes An.

    _____

    _____

3. my yesterday lost I pencil.

    _____

    _____

4. paint Kelly orange need Does?

    _____

    _____

5. the jump Harry wall Can over?

    _____

    _____

Name _____

Look at the second letter in each word. Number the words in ABC order.

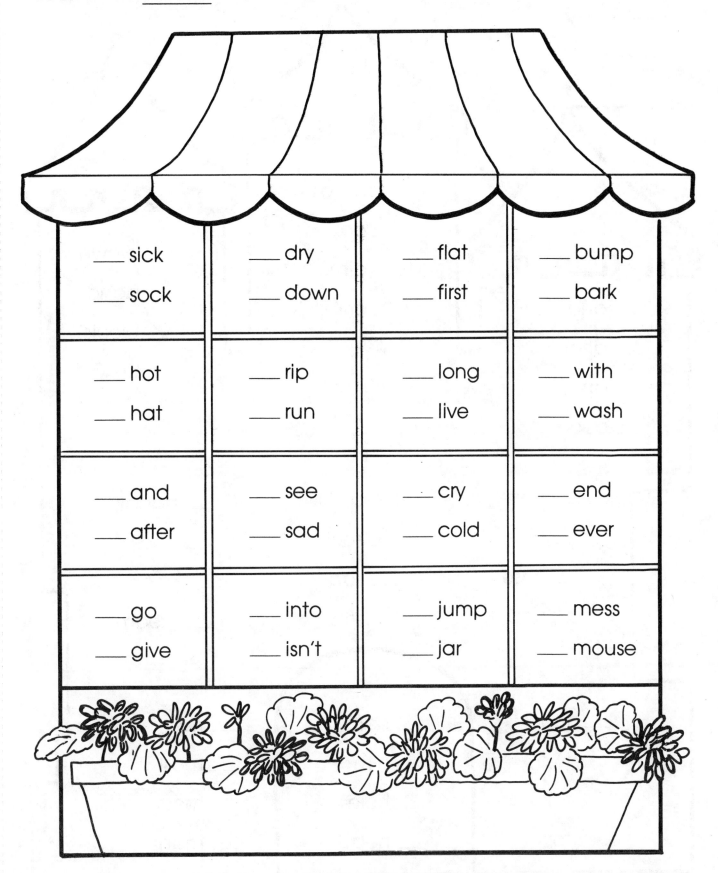

___ sick	___ dry	___ flat	___ bump
___ sock	___ down	___ first	___ bark
___ hot	___ rip	___ long	___ with
___ hat	___ run	___ live	___ wash
___ and	___ see	___ cry	___ end
___ after	___ sad	___ cold	___ ever
___ go	___ into	___ jump	___ mess
___ give	___ isn't	___ jar	___ mouse

Name _____ Alphabetizing

Look at the second letter in each word. Number the words in ABC order.

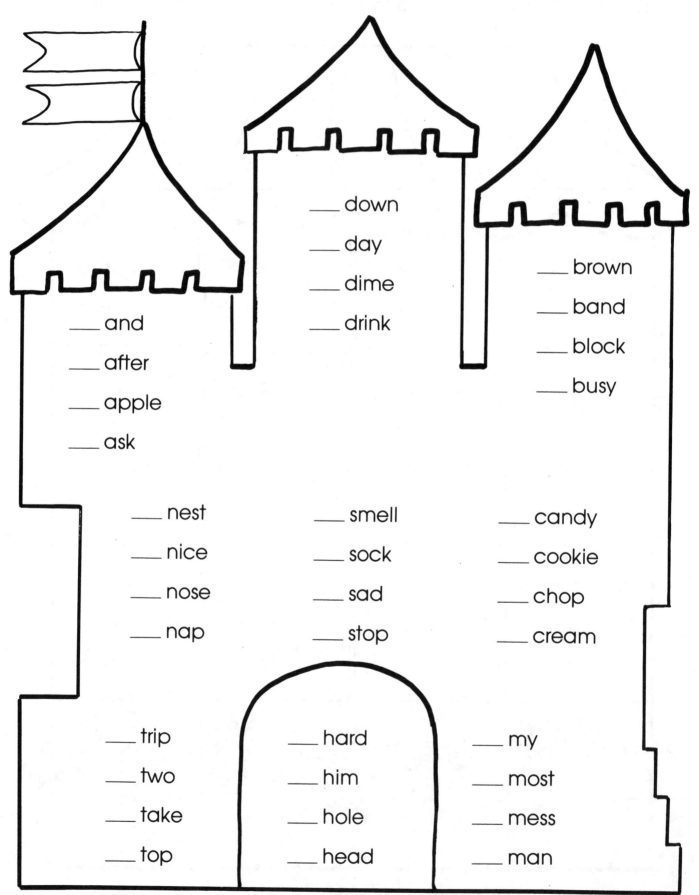

___ down
___ day
___ dime
___ drink

___ brown
___ band
___ block
___ busy

___ and
___ after
___ apple
___ ask

___ nest
___ nice
___ nose
___ nap

___ smell
___ sock
___ sad
___ stop

___ candy
___ cookie
___ chop
___ cream

___ trip
___ two
___ take
___ top

___ hard
___ him
___ hole
___ head

___ my
___ most
___ mess
___ man

18

Name _____ Alphabetizing

Look at the <u>second</u> letter in each word. Number them in ABC order.

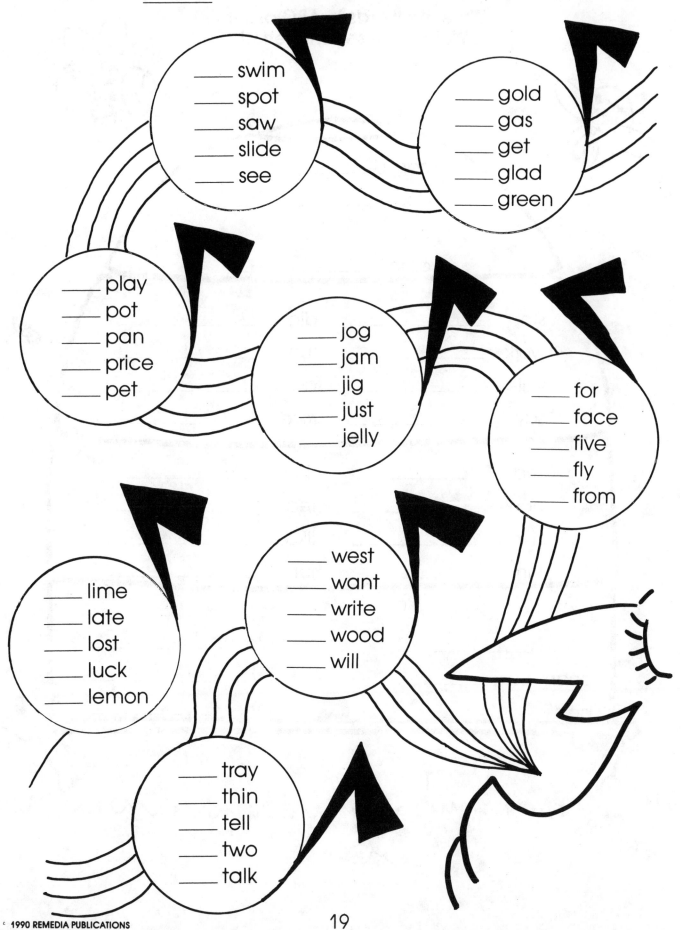

___ swim
___ spot
___ saw
___ slide
___ see

___ gold
___ gas
___ get
___ glad
___ green

___ play
___ pot
___ pan
___ price
___ pet

___ jog
___ jam
___ jig
___ just
___ jelly

___ for
___ face
___ five
___ fly
___ from

___ lime
___ late
___ lost
___ luck
___ lemon

___ west
___ want
___ write
___ wood
___ will

___ tray
___ thin
___ tell
___ two
___ talk

19

Write the words in ABC order.
Watch that second letter!

car _____

dog _____

come _____

drop _____

stop _____   dig _____

work _____   run _____

will _____   day _____

say _____   rose _____

may _____   rich _____

house _____   red _____

mice _____   like _____

him _____   let _____

inch _____   top _____

it _____   old _____

bean _____   over _____

bad _____   try _____

20

Number the words in ABC order. The words will make a sentence. Write the sentences on the lines.

1. ____ spots
    ____ dog
    ____ has
    ____ Ben's

2. ____ flew
    ____ Abe
    ____ kite
    ____ his

3. ____ five
    ____ Al
    ____ tacos
    ____ ate

4. ____ cherry
    ____ bakes
    ____ Annie
    ____ pies

5. ____ frog
    ____ Ed's
    ____ ugly
    ____ is

1. _____

2. _____

3. _____

4. _____

5. _____

Name _____

Number the words in ABC order.
Write the sentences.

1.
___ silly   ___ snakes
___ saw   ___ seven
___ I

2.
___ rose
___ my
___ Don't
___ red
___ drop

3.
___ old
___ Larry
___ socks
___ smelly
___ loves

4.
___ Duck
___ munchy
___ likes
___ quackers
___ Donald

5.
___ blew
___ A
___ bubbles
___ bear
___ bright

1. _____

2. _____

3. _____

4. _____

5. _____

22

a b c d e f g h	i j k l m n o p	q r s t u v w x y z
FIRST	**MIDDLE**	**LAST**

In which part of the alphabet are these letters? Write the word.

j _____

r _____

p _____

f _____

s _____

c _____

w _____

g _____

z _____

e _____

m _____

u _____

a b c d e f g h	i j k l m n o p	q r s t u v w x y z
FIRST	**MIDDLE**	**LAST**

In which part of the dictionary will you find these words?

step _____

cook _____

kite _____

now _____

fly _____

you _____

moth _____

zebra _____

anteater _____

lemon _____

open _____

button _____

Match:

water   first   ice   first

grab   middle   sink   middle

prize   last   dinner   last

24

Name _____   **Dictionary**

a b c d e f g h	i j k l m n o p	q r s t u v w x y z
FIRST	**MIDDLE**	**LAST**

1. Write the part where you will find these words.
2. Find them in your dictionary. Write the page number.

		Part	Page
1.	lark	_____	_____
2.	swine	_____	_____
3.	polar bear	_____	_____
4.	airport	_____	_____
5.	mammoth	_____	_____
6.	fig	_____	_____
7.	torch	_____	_____
8.	jaguar	_____	_____
9.	weed	_____	_____
10.	beetle	_____	_____

Write the part of the dictionary (first, middle, last) where you will find these words. Then find the word in your dictionary. Write the page number.

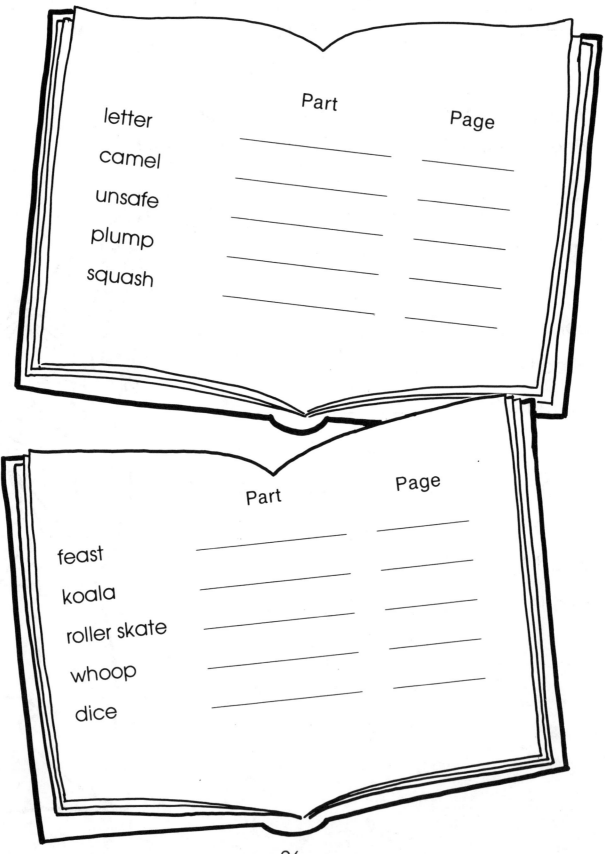

letter

camel

unsafe

plump

squash

Part

Page

feast

koala

roller skate

whoop

dice

Part

Page

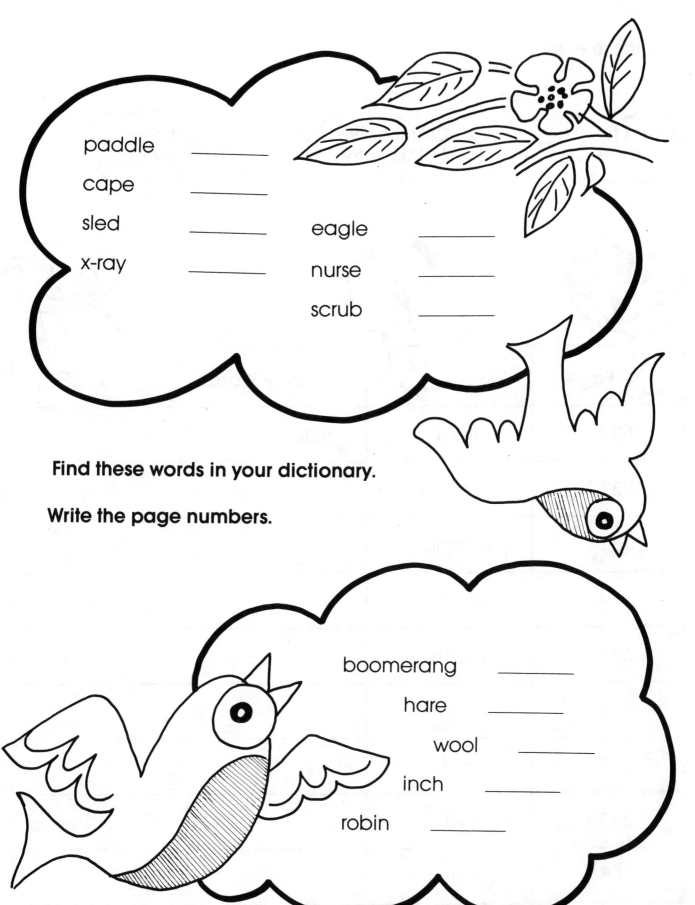

paddle   _____

cape   _____

sled   _____   eagle   _____

x-ray   _____   nurse   _____

                       scrub   _____

Find these words in your dictionary.

Write the page numbers.

boomerang   _____

hare   _____

wool   _____

inch   _____

robin   _____

Name _____

Find these <u>entry</u> words.

Open to this page.

Count down to this entry word.

Write the entry word here.

Page	Place	Entry Word
539	third	plain
731	seventh	
384	second	
19	tenth	
631	fourth	
175	fifth	
497	first	
313	sixth	
88	third	

**Find the entry word.
Write it.**

page 500
word 2
_____

page 212
word 5
_____

page 74
word 6
_____

page 28
word 1
_____

page 390
word 4
_____

page 653
word 7
_____

page 715
word 3
_____

page 139
word 4
_____

LOTS-O-
BUBBLES

What kind of word is it?

Find each entry word in your dictionary. Tell if it is a noun, verb, or adjective.

1. mug _____

2. hairless _____

3. spill _____

4. bridge _____

5. limp _____

6. pagoda _____

7. brew _____

8. sore _____

9. recess _____

10. needy _____

11. arise _____

12. bright _____

Use one noun in a sentence.

_____

_____

What kind of word is it?

noun	verb	adjective
goat | gōt | — *noun*	**pelt** | pĕlt | — *verb*	**hate • ful** | hāt′ fəl | — *adjective*

Find each entry word in your dictionary.
Tell if it is a noun, verb, or adjective.

1. bitter   _____

2. lift   _____

3. pinto   _____

4. tow   _____

5. fluffy   _____

6. chew   _____

7. impala   _____

8. salamander   _____

9. feeble   _____

10. jog   _____

11. curly   _____

12. adz   _____

Use one verb in a sentence.

_____

_____

Use your dictionary.
Find the entry word in dark letters.
Read the meaning.
Answer the question.

1. How many legs does a **fawn** have?

    _____

2. Where would you find an **andiron**?

    _____

3. What part of a boat is the **prow**?

    _____

4. Make a picture of something that grows in an **orchard**.

5. What would you do in a **berth**?

    _____

6. What is **wintergreen**? _____

    _____

7. When you **depart**, what do you say?

    _____

8. When would you wear **galoshes**?

    _____

Use your dictionary.
Find the word in dark letters.
Read the meaning. Answer the question.

1. Would an **adder** make a good pet? _____

   Why or why not? _____

   _____

2. Show what a **harpoon** looks like.

3. How many leaves does a **shamrock** have?   _____

4. Where would you use a **dinghy**?

   _____

5. Could you carry a **vat** in your pocket? _____

   Why or why not? _____

   _____

6. Where would you put a **brooch**?

   _____

   _____

7. What is a **heifer**?

   _____

   _____

8. What is a **knoll**?

   _____

   _____

Use your dictionary.
Find the word in dark letters.
Read the meaning.
Answer the question.

1. What color is a **coral** snake? _____

   _____

2. When do you say **adios**?

   _____

3. What is a **fang**?

   _____

4. Where is your **palate**?

   _____

5. How many legs does an **emu** have? _____

6. What would you find in a **moat**?

   _____

7. What does a **weather vane** tell you?

   _____

8. Could you keep a **bison** in your room? _____

   Why or why not? _____

   _____

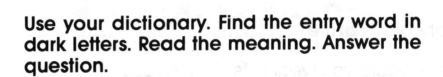

Use your dictionary. Find the entry word in dark letters. Read the meaning. Answer the question.

1. What do you need to see an **amoeba**?

    _____

2. What might make you feel **giddy**? _____

    _____

3. What color flowers does a **thistle** grow?

    _____

4. What could you find in a **belfry**?

    _____

5. What would you use to make a **notch**?

    _____

6. If you **capsize** your boat, what will happen to you?

    _____

7. Where do we get **sugar**?

    _____

8. What part of a **mallard** is green?

    _____

Use your dictionary. Find the word in dark letters. Read the meaning. Answer the question.

1. What color is **azure**? _____

2. Where would you wear a **fez**? _____

3. From where does **soot** come?

    _____

4. Where would you find **kelp**? _____

5. Should you eat **rhubarb** ? _____ Why or why not?

    _____

6. Who could have a **goatee**? _____

7. What color is the fur of an **ermine** in the winter?

    _____

8. Make a picture of you standing **akimbo**.

© 1990 REMEDIA PUBLICATIONS

Some words have more than one meaning.
Your dictionary will show you.

peep¹ |pēp| — *noun, plural* **peeps** A sound made by a young bird; chirp:
     We heard peeps coming from the robin's nest.

peep² |pēp| — *verb* **peeped, peeping** To look quickly or secretly:
     I peeped through the fence at the people next door.

Use your dictionary. Find the entry words in dark print. Read both meanings. Which one is used in the sentence? Write the number.

1.	**ring**	The bell will ring at 5 o'clock.	_____
2.	**hide**	We will hide the gold.	_____
3.	**bark**	Our dog will bark at you.	_____
4.	**duck**	The duck swam in the pond.	_____
5.	**mole**	He had a big mole on his arm.	_____
6.	**bat**	She hit the ball with the bat.	_____

Name _____   **Dictionary**

Find the entry word in your dictionary.
Read both meanings.
Tell which one is
used in the
sentence.

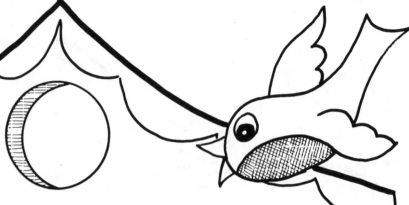

gob•ble¹ |gŏb' al| — *verb* **gobbled, gobbling** To eat quickly without chewing.

gob•ble² |gŏb' al| — *noun, plural* **gobbles** The sound made by a male turkey.

1. **bear**   I can't bear to look.   _____

2. **pen**   We keep our pig in a pen.   _____

3. **jar**   Here is a jar of jam.   _____

4. **hatch** We found a secret hatch in the wall.   _____

5. **date**   Dates taste very good.   _____

6. **sock**   The girl can't find her sock.   _____